MACHINE MANIA

WORKING VEHICLES

Frances Ridley

Copyright © ticktock Entertainment Ltd 2007
First published in Great Britain in 2007 by ticktock Media Ltd.,
Unit 2, Orchard Business Centre, North Farm Road,
Tunbridge Wells, Kent, TN2 3XF

ticktock project editor: Julia Adams
ticktock project designer: Emma Randall

We would like to thank: Alix Wood.

ISBN 978 1 84696 563 0

Printed in China
9 8 7 6 5 4 3 2

Picture credits:
b=bottom; c=centre; t=top; r=right; l=left
Alvey & Towers: 4-5c, 6-7c, b/c: cr; Caterpillar: 16-17c; Contruction Photo Library: 16cl; Corbis:
3b, 8-9c; JCB: 2t, 20-21, 21t, b/c: cl; John Deere: 22/23c, 23tr; Komatsu: 10-11c, 11t, 14-15c, 15t;
Letourneau Inc: 12-13c, 13t; Mack Trucks: 8cl; Oshkosh: 18-19c, 19t; Peterbilt: 4cl;

Every effort has been made to trace the copyright holders,
and we apologise in advance for any unintentional omissions.
We would be pleased to insert the appropriate acknowledgements
in any subsequent edition of this publication.

Contents

Peterbilt 379 Road Truck 4

Mercedes-Benz Actros 6

Mack Road Train 8

Haulpak 930E Dump Truck 10

LeTourneau L-2350 Wheel Loader 12

Komatsu D575A Super Dozer 14

CAT 385L Excavator 16

Oshkosh S-Series Mixer Truck 18

JCB Backhoe Loader 20

John Deere 9750 Combine 22

Glossary 24

Peterbilt 379 Road Truck

The Peterbilt 379 Road Truck is an **articulated** truck. This means it is made up of two parts: a **tractor unit** and a **trailer**.

The Peterbilt weighs 12 tonnes. It carries 25 tonnes of cargo. It needs a massive engine. The engine is under a long **hood** at the front of the truck.

Mercedes-Benz Actros

The Mercedes-Benz Actros is a cabover truck. This means the driver's cab is over the engine.

Cabover trucks take up less space on the road. Actros trucks can carry 29 tonnes of goods. They carry everything from milk to racing cars!

Actros cabs are very comfortable for long journeys. The cabs are **soundproofed**. This keeps out engine noise.

Mack Road Train

Road trains are trucks that pull three or more **trailers**. Mack is famous for making road trains. All Mack trucks have a bulldog mascot on the **hood**.

The biggest Mack truck is called the Titan. It is 53 metres long. It carries huge loads between cities. It has four fuel tanks and a huge **radiator** to cool its engine down.

Haulpak 930E Dump Truck

Dump trucks carry heavy loads on building sites. They don't go on roads.

The Haulpak 930E dump truck is huge. Its wheels are nearly 3 metres tall. The driver climbs a ladder to get into the cab!

10

The Haulpak works in quarries and mines.
It carries rock, earth and coal. Its **bucket** is
made of **steel**. Six big cars could fit in the bucket!

930E

LeTourneau L-2350 Wheel Loader

A wheel loader digs up earth and rocks in its **bucket**. Then it dumps them into the back of a truck.

The driver sits in the cab. He uses a **joystick** to make the bucket dig and dump.

The LeTourneau L-2350 wheel loader
is huge. A car could fit into its bucket.
Its tyres are four metres tall – taller than
three children put together!

Komatsu D575A Super Dozer

Bulldozers break up earth and push it around. The Komatsu D575A Super Dozer is huge. It is two times bigger than any other bulldozer.

The Super Dozer has special tracks. They help it ride over muddy or bumpy ground.

The Super Dozer has a Super Ripper!
It breaks up 2,000 tonnes of earth an hour.

Cat 385L Excavator

The Cat 385L Excavator is a huge digging machine. It weighs 83.5 tonnes.

Its bright colour is called 'Highway yellow'. It stands out well from other traffic.

The 385L has a long arm with a **bucket** on the end. The bucket scoops up soil and dumps it into a truck. The driver sits in the cab. He can turn the cab all the way round.

Oshkosh S-Series Mixer Truck

The Oshkosh S-Series Mixer Truck carries 6 tonnes of sand, 6 tonnes of gravel and 1.5 tonnes of cement. It mixes them to make concrete.

The Oshkosh mixes the concrete in its **drum**. The drum turns round slowly as the Oshkosh travels along.

At the building site, the drum turns round the other way. This pushes the concrete to out. The concrete comes down a **chute**.

JCB Backhoe Loader

The JCB Backhoe Loader has a **bucket** to dig trenches. It also has an arm with a **shovel** on the end. This picks up the earth and moves it away.

You can choose the size of bucket you want when you buy a JCB. You can say how long the arm should be, too.

JCB has a team of Dancing Diggers!
They do stunts and shows.

John Deere 9750 Combine

John Deere make lots of machines for farms. The company's badge shows a deer.

The 9750 Combine harvests ripe wheat. It cuts the wheat down and strips the grain from the stalks. It stores the grain in a tank and leaves the stalks behind.

It takes one day for ten men
to harvest a small field.
It takes the 9750 Combine
one hour!

Glossary

Articulated   A truck in two parts.

Bucket   The scoop of a digging machine.

Chute   A slide to take things from one place to another.

Drum   The part of a truck that mixes concrete.

Hood   The metal door over the engine.

Joystick   A lever you use to control a machine.

Radiator   Part of a vehicle that helps cool the engine down.

Shovel   A scoop used to lift and throw rocks and earth.

Soundproofed   A way of making noise quieter.

Steel   A Strong metal.

Tractor unit   The tractor's cab, engine and front wheels.

Trailer   The container with wheels that the tractor or truck pulls along.